A Very Merry

DUNDER MIFFLIN

Christmas

Running Press
Hachette Book Group
1290 Avenue of the Americas, New York, NY 10104
www.runningpress.com
@Running_Press

Printed in Canada

First Edition: October 2020

Published by Running Press, an imprint of Perseus Books, LLC, a subsidiary of Hachette Book Group, Inc. The Running Press name and logo is a trademark of the Hachette Book Group.

The Hachette Speakers Bureau provides a wide range of authors for speaking events. To find out more, go to www.hachettespeakersbureau.com or call (866) 376-6591.

The publisher is not responsible for websites (or their content) that are not owned by the publisher.

Print book cover and interior design by Celeste Joyce.

Library of Congress Control Number: 2020935768

ISBNs: 978-0-7624-9836-9 (hardcover), 978-0-7624-7216-1 (ebook)

FRI

10   9   8   7   6   5   4   3   2   1

A Very Merry
DUNDER
MIFFLIN
Christmas

Celebrating the Holidays with the Office

Christine Kopaczewski

RUNNING PRESS
PHILADELPHIA

DUNDER
MIFFLIN, INC.
PAPER COMPANY

1725 SLOUGH AVENUE
SCRANTON, PA 18505

CONTENTS

INTRODUCTION

OVER the course of seven epic Christmas episodes, *The Office* delighted audiences everywhere with unconventional, often outrageous, and seriously funny memories. Each December, ready to blow off a year's worth of pent-up boredom and frustration, the hyped-up holiday party was the ultimate escape from the team's monotonous paper-pushing gigs and the perfect recipe for chaos, love triangles, and prank wars to ensue . . . and they did.

In the pages ahead, you'll relive your favorite festive moments, get tips on planning your own seasonal soiree, find the perfect gift for that special someone, and a slew of other holiday hacks and high jinks. So, before you dive into forming your own Party Planning Committee, let's look back at all the ways Michael and his workmates at Dunder Mifflin made the most of their holiday seasons.

HOW DUNDER MIFFLIN DOES THE HOLIDAYS

If Jim and Dwight are up to their old pranks again, if Michael is committing another party faux pas, it must be the holidays at Dunder Mifflin. Ahead are crib notes to all seven unforgettable Christmas episodes and a Dunder Mifflin Christmas quiz to test your *Office* knowledge.

CHRISTMAS EPISODE CRIB NOTES

Christmas Party

SEASON 2

Ryan: "Angela drafted me into the Party Planning Committee. Her memo said that we need to prepare for every possible disaster. Which to me seems excessive."

The first of the Christmas episodes set the tone for the seasons of holiday hilarity that followed. Without consulting the almighty Party Planning Committee, Michael decides to arrange a Secret Santa for everyone to participate in. Although there's a $20 limit on all Secret Santa gifts, Michael blatantly ignores the rules and splurges on a video iPod (dropping at least $400) for Ryan.

Dwight: "Okay, everybody, listen up! It is time to get your presents, wrap them, and place them under the tree like so. If you do not get your present wrapped and under the tree within the next five minutes, you will be disqualified from Secret Santa. All right? No exceptions except Michael."

3

Jim is excited to learn that he's gotten Pam as his Secret Santa and fills a teapot with meaningful trinkets and a card revealing his feelings for her. Dwight, decked out as one of Santa's elves, gathers the group around the tree to get the festivities started. However, things quickly take a turn for the worse when Michael is furious to find that he's received a handmade oven mitt from Phyllis. In hopes of getting a gift more suited to his taste, he insists that the group play Yankee Swap.

Dwight: "Yankee Swap is like Machiavelli meets . . . Christmas."

Things continue to spiral when gifts suited specifically for one person, like a name-plate engraved with KELLY (obviously meant for Kelly Kapoor) and Jim's special teapot for Pam, are being shifted around from colleague to colleague, all trying to trade up for Michael's iPod.

Michael: "Everyone wants the iPod. It's a huge hit. It is almost a Christmas miracle."

In the end, Pam claims the iPod as her own and Jim is distraught to find that Dwight has taken the teapot to clean out his sinuses. Pam, however, has a change of heart when her fiancé Roy tells her that he was going to get her an iPod for Christmas anyway and is out of good gift ideas. She trades and gets the teapot back from Dwight, telling Jim that she did so because of all the effort he put in to spare his feelings.

Michael: "I want people to cut loose. I want people making out in closets. I want people hanging from the ceilings, lamp shades on the heads. I want it to be a Playboy Mansion party. And also I want you to spread the word that I will have my digital camera. And I'll be taking pictures all along the way."

Meanwhile, Michael is annoyed by the night's turn of events, and buys 15 bottles of vodka, despite a strict alcohol-free party policy. The entire group (minus Angela) drinks and is merry, until a very intoxicated Meredith flashes Michael.

Kevin: "Why did you get it so big?"

Michael: "A, that's what she said, and B, I wanted it to be impressive. The biggest day of the year deserves the biggest tree of the year."

Kevin: "But what are we going to do with this hacked-off part?"

Michael: "Well, that is a perfectly good mini-tree, Kevin. And we are going to sell that to charity. That's what Christmas is all about."

Benihana Christmas

SEASON 3

> **Michael:** "This is an old adage, but they say when you find true love, you know within the first 24 hours. With Carol, I knew within the first 24 minutes of the second day I met her."

Season 3's holiday gathering hits a bit of a snag when Michael is suddenly dumped by his girlfriend, Carol. Lonely and stuck with a romantic couples getaway to Sandals (Michael's gift to Carol), he mopes around the office all day—until Andy moves into action to put a smile back on Michael's face. His fix? A trip to Benihana. Andy and Jim insist that Michael accompany them to what they fondly call "Japanese Hooters," and hilarity follows.

Michael: "I'd like everybody's attention. Christmas is canceled."

Stanley: "You can't cancel a holiday."

Michael: "Keep it up, Stanley, and you will lose New Year's."

Stanley: "What does that mean?"

Michael: "Jim, take New Year's away from Stanley."

7

Andy and Michael spend their time drinking nog-a-sakes and flirting with the waitresses, while Dwight regales the chef with his knowledge of Japanese knives.

Ryan: "I miss the days when there was only one party I didn't want to go to."

Back at the office, things aren't so copacetic. There's an uprising among the Party Planning Committee and a new committee forms—the Committee to Plan Parties, run by Pam and Karen. Dueling party themes divide the office. Angela has planned a classic *Nutcracker* theme, complete with sweets, treats, and a Tchaikovsky soundtrack, and forces Phyllis into giving her a hand.

Kevin: "I think I'll go to Angela's party, because that's the party I know."

Meanwhile, Pam and Karen have planned a Margarita and Karaoke Christmas, naturally the more popular theme for the Dunder Mifflin group. While the tequila and good times flow, Pam starts to feel slightly guilty about outshining Angela's event. She asks to merge parties, and after a little convincing, Angela agrees.

Dwight: [to Pam and Karen] "You must turn over to me all Christmas decorations and party paraphernalia immediately that will be returned to you on January 4."

By this point, Dwight, Michael, Andy, and Jim have returned with two waitresses from Benihana, one of whom Michael introduces as his new girlfriend. After a few drinks, Michael invites one of the waitresses to Jamaica, trying to sweeten the deal by offering her the bike he ostentatiously put in the children's gift box earlier. She declines his invitation, but accepts the bike and pedals away. A forlorn Michael is consoled by Jim, who explains that he just successfully survived his first rebound.

Michael: "Bros before hos. Why? Because your bros are always there for you. They have got your back after your ho rips your heart out for no good reason. And you were nothing but great to your ho and you told her she was the only ho for you. And that she was better than all the other hos in the world. And then . . . and then suddenly she's not yo' ho no mo'."

Phyllis: "Oh, I don't think it's blackmail. Angela just does what I ask her to do so I won't tell everyone that she's cheating on Andy with Dwight. I think for it to be blackmail it would have to be a formal letter."

Widely considered the most popular Christmas episode, season 5's holiday special does not disappoint. After seeing Angela cheat on Andy with Dwight, Phyllis has gained control of the Party Planning Committee (by blackmailing Angela) and is going all out on the theme—a Moroccan Christmas. There's authentic Moroccan cuisine, hookahs, sitars, floor seating, and a buffet of alcoholic beverages.

Andy: [sitting on floor playing the sitar] "Hey, hey . . . Ange . . . check it out. There's a place in France where the naked ladies dance."
Angela: "Really, Andy? It's Christmas and you're singing about nudity and France."

Meredith hits the open bar a little too hard and sets herself on fire while belly-dancing to Andy's sitar playing. Dwight steps into action and promptly puts the flames out with a fire extinguisher, bringing all the fun to a screeching halt.

Andy: "When I was in college, I used to get wicked hammered. My nickname was puke."

Michael decides it's time to stage an intervention and sits the whole office down so they can share with Meredith how her alcoholism affects them. At the end of the party, he traps an unwilling Meredith and attempts to drop her off at a rehabilitation center against her will.

Michael: "You know what's the only thing I want for Christmas? I want Meredith to get better. That's my only wish. But you know what? My wishes never come true, so I'm not going to wish that on her. I . . . a watch would be nice."

Meanwhile, Dwight and Jim are in the midst of one of their usual prank wars. This spar starts with Dwight's gift-wrapped desk. Assuming that Jim has merely wrapped his seat in paper, he plops down to find that Jim has actually replaced his entire desk and chair set with cardboard, and promptly collapses to the ground. But, in true Dwight fashion, he doesn't let his embarrassing fall get him down. He's got bigger plans, like selling off dozens of the season's hottest toy—Princess Unicorn—for $200 a pop to desperate parents.

Each year, Dwight hits up the local toy stores, buys their entire stock of the season's most popular present, and scams people into purchasing them for an outrageously high price tag. Jim is shocked to discover how well it works, even on Toby and Darryl.

Phyllis: "I was waiting until later to hand out this year's gifts from corporate. *[holds up shot glass]* I don't think they're appropriate anymore."

The episode ends with a shocker: Phyllis reveals to the whole office that Angela has been cheating on Andy, after Angela defies Phyllis's commands. Everyone's speechless, except for Andy, who just happened to be out of the room when the announcement was made.

Secret Santa
SEASON 6

Phyllis: "I have been wanting to be Santa for years. I believe I have the right temperament and the figure to do the job well. I slipped a note to Jim eleven weeks ago and he said I could do it. It's been a long journey . . . but I'm Santa Claus!"

In season 6's holiday episode, Phyllis decides to become the office Santa and dresses up as the big man herself. She does have the right figure and temperament (as she says), after all. This, of course, does not go unnoticed by Michael, who is furious that someone would attempt to steal his Santa suit thunder. He decides to one-up her by turning his jacket inside out and morphing into the ultimate icon of Christmas—Jesus Christ.

Michael: "Behold! Jesus Christ. And I bring to you glad Christmas tidings. I want to remind everyone of the true meaning of Christmas. Those of you who wish to join me, that's great. I'm excited by that. And those of you who don't, I forgive you. But I never forget."

Michael causes a scene, interrupting Phyllis as she hands out Secret Santa gifts and claims that Jesus can heal leopards. When Jim forces Michael to stop, he heads into his office to sulk and call CFO David Wallace to complain. David tells Michael that someone has purchased the company and, presumably, he and everyone else will lose their jobs. Michael, shocked and upset, decides to call a meeting right in the middle of the party.

Jim: "You can't yell out, 'I need this, I need this,' as you pin down an employee on your lap!"
Michael: "Okay. You know what, Jim, there are two Santas in the room. Things get ruthless!"

While Michael's Santa/Jesus crisis is unraveling, Erin is dealing with a bit of a crisis herself—some monster keeps sending her items from "The 12 Days of Christmas." After her cat kills the turtledove and the French hens have started to pull her hair out to build a nest, she begs for the madness to stop. An extremely lovesick Andy, who has a mega crush on Erin, is anxious and upset to learn that his well-planned Secret Santa gift for her has gone so awry. He begs Phyllis to keep it a secret that he was the one sending Erin the 12 days of Christmas.

Phyllis: "In the North Pole, I spend many nights alone tinkering with toys. So today, let's put a twinkle in Ole Kris Kringle's eye! Let the party begin!"

Dwight also has a complicated gifting scenario to sort out himself. For several weeks someone has been sending him small pieces to assemble, of what he assumes is a gun. After struggling for days, Michael gives him a small hint that helps him realize it's not a gun, but a nutcracker!

Back in Michael's impromptu meeting, he shares with the group the grim news that they will soon be unemployed. After a suspicious Jim asks for confirmation, Michael calls David again, who informs him that he meant only upper management—like the CEO and executives—would be let go. Relieved, everyone rejoices over drinks and dances to the sweet sounds of 12 drummers drumming, Andy's final gift to Erin.

Michael: "You know what, Christmas isn't about Santa, or Jesus. It's about the workplace. All of you feel like my family. Ryan, you are my son. And Pam, you're my wife. And Jim. And Angela and Phyllis, you are my Grandmas. And Stanley, you're our mailman."

Creed: "What if you've been bad?"

Phyllis: "Oh, then nothing but a lump of coal for you!"

Creed: "What if you've been really, really bad? More evil, and strictly wrong?"

Jim: "Hey, Creed, we covered it. Lump of coal!"

Pam: "I'm the office administrator now, which means I'm basically being paid to be head of the Party Planning Committee. The first thing I did as head . . . I shut it down. At its best, it was a toxic political club used to make others feel miserable and left out. At its best, it planned parties."

Things are chugging along—business as usual—for the holiday party this year. The Party Planning Committee's been disbanded, keeping any unnecessary drama at bay. Things can't stay calm for long, though, and Michael's thrown into a tizzy and demands an entirely new party after receiving some shocking news. His former flame, Holly, is transferring back to the Scranton office to cover for Toby while he's on jury duty for the Scranton Strangler case.

Stanley: "I have been trying to get on jury duty every single year since I was 18 years old. To get to go sit in an air-conditioned room downtown, judging people while my lunch is paid for . . . that is the life."

Suddenly, the group's traditional office party isn't nearly good enough for fancy New Hampshire–based Holly. As Michael puts it, "Someone from New Hampshire looks at a fake tree and sees a burning cross." He trashes the food, décor, and dishes from the original party plan, and insists that everyone up their game. Holly arrives to a sophisticated soiree, complete with champagne, jazz music, and fancy finger foods.

Michael: "Man, I worked hard. I worked so hard for this! I was after corporate constantly. I emailed Joe. I wrote letters. And, know who I end up owing this to? The Scranton Strangler. Thank you. Thank you, Scranton Strangler. I love you! You just took one more person's breath away."

But Dunder Mifflin can't have nice things going on for long—Jim breaks a window during a petty snowball fight with Dwight, causing a frigid breeze to burst through the office, and Holly tells Michael that she's still in a relationship with A.J. (which obviously does not go over well).

A spiraling Michael tells Holly that he has a girlfriend in New York named Tara (he does not), throws her *Toy Story* Woody doll that was gifted to her from A.J. in the trash, and breaks down to Pam. To lift his spirits, Pam breaks girl code and tells Michael a secret Holly confided to the girls. She's given A.J. an ultimatum to propose within a year. Michael returns to the party with renewed hope.

While Michael's love saga sweeps through the office, Darryl's dealing with his own broken heart when he learns that his daughter, Jada, doesn't want to spend Christmas with him this year. To win her over, Pam and Andy devise a plan to make this classy Christmas party kid-friendly. Andy dresses up as the Grinch and sets up the world's shortest scavenger hunt for Jada to find the Christmas star he's stolen from atop the office tree. Jada's disappointed and Darryl's feeling more stressed by the minute, trying to make it a memorable holiday for her. Things take a turn for the better, however, when he takes her into the breakroom and she's wowed by the impressive display of vending machine snacks. She buys them all and shares her treasures with the rest of the office.

Meanwhile, Jim and Dwight take a break from their snowball fight while Pam presents Jim with her homemade gift. She created a comic book based on a character named Jimmy Halpert, who's been bitten by a radioactive bear and gains its superpowers. Jim loves it, despite the harsh criticism Pam's received from countless coworkers. Jim reciprocates with a truly stunning diamond tennis bracelet.

Jim: "I surrender."

Dwight: "I do not accept your surrender. There's only one way that I would ever relent."

Jim: "Anything. You got it."

Dwight: "You hit Pam in the face with a snowball while I watch."

Jim: "You're a psychopath."

Dwight: "I'll take that as a no."

But the holiday happiness only lasts for so long when a worn-down Jim concedes defeat in the snowball fight, and, in an unprecedented move, Dwight actually wins the prank war against Jim. Dwight, of course, doesn't let him down that easy. On his way out to his car, Jim's met with dozens of snowmen in the parking lot. Assuming that Dwight's hidden himself inside one of them, Jim goes nuts trying to destroy them all. The camera pans up to reveal Dwight on the roof of the building watching, satisfied at the fear and paranoia he's unleashed. He turns and wishes the camera a "Merry Christmas."

Dwight: "In the end, the greatest snowball isn't a snowball at all. It's fear. Merry Christmas."

Christmas Wishes

SEASON 8

In the first Christmas episode after Michael's move to Colorado with his fiancée, Holly, Andy takes on the role of manager and office Santa. In an effort to keep things cheery, despite missing Michael, he asks the employees to give him their biggest Christmas wish, which he'll attempt to grant. This proves harder than he initially thought, when a very intoxicated Erin asks him to murder and bury his new girlfriend, Jessica (whom he's brought to the holiday party).

Erin: "I love Jessica, and I haven't even met her yet. It's like we don't even need to meet, you know? I already love you. Stay home."

Dwight and Jim are partaking in their traditional holiday high jinks, but their usual office antics are disrupted when Cathy, their new desk mate, files a complaint about their constant shenanigans. Andy tells the guys that the next one to pull a prank will lose his Christmas bonus to the victim of the prank. Seeing green, both Dwight and Jim attempt to frame each other by pulling pranks or tempting the other to make a move.

Jim: "Dwight really wants my bonus. He's trying to entrap me. Oh, God, now I can't drink at this thing . . . I get really pranky when I drink."

Jim shouts his credit card information for all to hear, hoping Dwight will buy something. The plan backfires, though, when Dwight uses the details to send Pam a $200 bouquet of flowers.

Dwight then pricks himself with a porcupine needle, claiming to the office that Jim left the animal in his desk drawer. No one bites and the tit-for-tat continues when Jim, uncharacteristically, defaces a photo of his baby daughter Cece and blames Dwight. An upset Andy thinks Dwight has gone too far and tells Jim this vandalism is grounds for dismissal. An embarrassed Jim admits to defacing the image on his own. Andy tells Jim that he won't touch their bonuses, but their behavior can no longer affect their or any other colleague's work performance. Jim, however, neglects to tell

Dwight the news and Dwight continues to prank himself by spray-painting DWIGHT SUCKS on his own car, hoping to convince everyone else that Jim did it.

As the party ends, Andy's off to fulfill Meredith's Christmas wish, serving as her designated driver home, when he realizes how worried he is about Erin. Having left with a newly divorced Robert Indiana, Andy follows them home, only to witness Robert being the perfect gentleman, seeing Erin to her door, and offering several words of encouragement. Andy drives away with a smile on his face.

Dwight Christmas
SEASON 9

Erin: "Oh, hey, guys, the Christmas party is today. Merry Christmas everyone!"

Angela: "No."

Nellie: "Is It?"

Erin: "I mean, it says 'X-Mas party,' but I think we all know what that's code for."

In season 9's memorable holiday episode, Dwight takes it upon himself to spread some Christmas cheer after realizing that the Party Planning Committee has neglected to plan an event this year. The catch? He will only host the holiday party if his colleagues agree to his theme—a traditional Pennsylvania Dutch Christmas, akin to the ones he had growing up. After a series of moans, groans, and flat-out no's, Pam convinces her coworkers to give Dwight a shot.

Pam: "We're the Party Planning Committee, and we did not get where we are by playing it safe. We got here by being risk takers. And, yeah, Dwight's party is gonna be terrible. Maybe. Maybe it's not. Maybe it's going to be great. And if it's great . . . I think we all know what that would mean to us."

Phyllis: "Let's do it!"

Pam: "Yes! Phyllis!"

Angela: "No. I don't want my name attached to this party."

Pam: "What does that even mean? Where would your name appear?"

Angela: "Please just take my name off of everything."

Dwight launches into action, dressing up as the crotchety, fur-clad German Christmas figure, Belsnickel, prepares German food, and oversees a game similar to Naughty versus Nice. Everyone is miserable except for Pam and Jim, who relish another chance to laugh at Dwight.

Jim decides to leave Dwight's German holiday shindig early to get to Philadelphia for his new job the next day. Everyone's upset, especially Dwight. The most distraught, though, is Darryl. Weeks ago, Jim had promised Darryl a job in Philly, but neglects to mention it again before his departure. Darryl starts to drink heavily and plots to punch Jim in the face when he sees him again.

While the rest of the office is being judged as "impish or admirable" by Belsnickel (Dwight), intern Pete is teaching Erin about a different kind of Christmas tradition—*Die Hard*. Andy Bernard, her boyfriend and former Dunder Mifflin employee, is still away sailing on his family's boat—leaving her feeling a little glum around the holidays this year. Pete works to cheer Erin up by reciting the entire movie from memory, which

she compares against an online transcript. It's not funny enough to keep her emotions fully at bay, though, and she winds up breaking down and crying. Pete puts his arm around her and Erin tells him to keep it there.

Meanwhile, Toby's in the kitchen, regaling Nellie Bartram with stories about his time on the Scranton Strangler jury. Tired of his nonstop talking, she kisses him to shut him up. He pauses and passionately kisses her back.

Dwight: "Party's over. You quit on Christmas, Christmas quits on you. And guess what, kids? Belsnickel isn't real. It's me, Dwight!"

Just as the party's winding down, Jim returns, much to Darryl's chagrin. Just as Darryl is stumbling over to confront him, Jim turns and tells him that he's put in a good word for Darryl and has arranged for him to have an interview. Darryl, appeased but extremely intoxicated, turns around and passes out on the catering table, causing it to collapse around him. And to all a good night!

Phyllis: "We found some old decorations in the warehouse. Oscar ran to the store for some food and drink, and I dipped into my stash of eggnog. I guess they needed me after all."

QUIZ: HOW WELL DO YOU KNOW CHRISTMAS AT DUNDER MIFFLIN?

1. What was inside the teapot that Jim gave Pam?

    A. Boggle timer
    B. Golf pencil
    C. Jim's high school photo
    D. Hot sauce packet

2. What song do Andy and Michael perform as a karaoke duet?

    A. "Take a Chance on Me"
    B. "You Sexy Thing"
    C. "Your Body Is a Wonderland"
    D. "Ryan Started the Fire"

3. What Secret Santa gift did Phyllis handmake for Michael that he wasn't happy with?

    A. Oven mitt
    B. Bobblehead
    C. A portrait of him done by memory
    D. A Dundie for Best Boss

4. What is the name of Andy's girlfriend—the one he brings to the Christmas party (much to Erin's dismay)?

    A. Jessica
    B. Jasmine
    C. Julia
    D. Belsnickel

5. Pam's comic book for Jim, *The Adventures of Jimmy Halpert,* stars a _____ , who while riding his bike through the woods is bitten by a radioactive _____ , causing Jim to become _____ , resulting in him wreaking havoc on the office.

    A. A hyper vigilant salesman/farmer/martial arts expert; Polluticorn; Recyclops
    B. An awesome paper salesman; Andy Bernard; Big Tuna
    C. A mild-mannered salesman; bear; Bear Man
    D. A super-annoying HR person; something horrible; who cares

6. Which celebrity does drunk Darryl compare Meredith to?

    A. Emma Stone
    B. Amy Adams
    C. Kathy Bates
    D. Will Ferrell

7. According to Angela, what color is whorish?

    A. Red
    B. Black
    C. Green
    D. Orange

8. What pattern is on the paper Jim uses to wrap Dwight's desk?

    A. Reindeer
    B. Christmas trees
    C. Snowflakes
    D. Plain red

9. What was Andy Bernard's nickname in college?

    A. Ace
    B. Buzz
    C. Nard Dog
    D. Boner Champ

10. What kind of cookies did Phyllis serve at her Moroccan Christmas party?

    A. Halwa chebakia
    B. Macaroons
    C. Ktefa
    D. Baghrir

ANSWER KEY

1. All of the above

2. **C.** "Your Body Is a Wonderland"

3. **A.** Oven mitt

4. **A.** And Erin wishes she were dead.

5. **C.** Pam's comic book for Jim, *The Adventures of Jimmy Halpert*, stars a mild-mannered salesman, who while riding his bike through the woods is bitten by a radioactive bear, causing Jim to become Bear Man, resulting in him wreaking havoc on the office.

6. **A.** Emma Stone . . . he was *very* drunk.

7. **C.** and **D.** Angela considers red and black more satanic than whorish.

8. **B.** Christmas trees

9. All of the above

10. **A.** Halwa chebakia, a traditional cookie served during Ramadan, made with sesame seeds and honey. Stanley says, "Mmm, chewy." Angela spits hers out.

HOSTING THE HOLIDAYS DUNDER MIFFLIN–STYLE

By now your Party Planning Committee is hard at work and the office tree is ready to be decorated. Here are the best party themes, dishes, and drinks to host the ultimate office Christmas party and tips for tree trimming.

Michael: "Happy Birthday, Jesus. Sorry your party's so lame."

PARTIES, PLAYLISTS, AND MEMORABLE HOLIDAY DISHES

Meredith: "We're out there sweating our balls off every day, bustin' our balls. We deserve a Christmas party!"

A Nutcracker Christmas

Nothing says classic Christmas like a little Tchaikovsky. Put on your matching turtleneck and sweater set and get ready to party.

Supplies

*   Party streamers

*   Green clothes only

*   Nutcrackers (of course)

*   A tree

*   Garland

Menu

*   Angela's Double-Fudge Brownies (see page 47)

*   Mixed nuts (walnuts, peanuts, hazelnuts, pecans, and Brazil nuts)

*   Fruit punch (nonalcoholic)

Playlist

The Nutcracker Suite by Tchaikovsky

"The Dance of the Sugar Plum Fairy" (on repeat)

"The Little Drummer Boy" by Katherine Kennicott Davis (choir pose encouraged—just take inspiration from Angela)

Angela's Double-Fudge Brownies

Kevin: "I hear Angela's party will have double-fudge brownies. It will also have Angela."

¾ cup baking cocoa
½ teaspoon baking soda
⅔ cup melted butter, divided
½ cup boiling water
2 cups sugar
2 large eggs

1 ½ cups all-purpose flour
1 teaspoon vanilla extract
¼ teaspoon salt
2 cups (12 ounces) semisweet
chocolate chunks

Preheat the oven to 350°F. Combine the cocoa and baking soda.

Blend ⅓ cup melted butter. Add boiling water; stir until well blended.

Slowly add the sugar, eggs, and the remaining butter. Next, add flour, vanilla, and salt. Stir in the chocolate chunks.

Pour into a greased 9 by 13-inch baking pan and bake 35 to 40 minutes. Let them cool so the Kevin in your life doesn't burn his tongue.

Margarita Karaoke Christmas

For the fun-loving crowd, you'll only need two things to get the party started—a margarita mixer and a karaoke machine.

Supplies

* Margarita machine

* Margarita glasses

* Salt (for the rim)

* Karaoke machine

* Christmas drinking games

Menu

* Margaritas

* Chips with salsa

* Guacamole and queso

* Kevin's Dreaded Mini Cupcakes (see page 50)

Playlist

A solid mix of the seventies, eighties, nineties, and now. For starters:

"Your Body Is a Wonderland" by John Mayer
(office bros Michael and Andy duet this
John Mayer classic)

"We Belong" by Pat Benatar

"Spinnin' N Reelin'" by Creed Bratton
(an '80s uptempo tune is always a good idea,
according to Creed)

"Lady" by Styx (Dwight sings this to Angela)

Kevin's Dreaded Mini Cupcakes

Kevin: "Mini cupcakes? As in the mini version of regular cupcakes, which is already a mini version of regular cake? Honestly, where does it end with you people?!"

1 cup all-purpose flour
1 teaspoon baking powder
¼ teaspoon salt
⅓ cup whole milk
½ teaspoon vanilla extract
6 tablespoons unsalted butter, softened
½ cup plus 1 tablespoon sugar
1 large egg
1 ¾ cups vanilla buttercream frosting
2 mini muffin pans, each with 24 (1 ¾-inch) muffin cups
24 foil or paper mini muffin liners

Preheat the oven to 350°F. Place liners in the muffin cups.

Whisk together the flour, baking powder, and salt in a bowl. In a separate small bowl, stir together the milk and vanilla.

In a large bowl, beat the butter and sugar at medium-high speed with an electric mixer until pale and fluffy, about 4 minutes. Add the egg and reduce the mixer speed to low. Begin adding the flour and milk mixtures alternately.

Divide the batter among the muffin cups, filling them two-thirds full, and bake until the tops are golden. Insert a wooden toothpick into the center of a cupcake. If it comes out clean, they are done. Let them cool completely, then top with frosting before serving.

Benihana Christmas

Take the party outside the office for a change of pace.

Supplies

* None. Let the good folks at Benihana do what they do best.

Menu

* Nog-a-Sakes (see page 55)

* Sake bombs

* Hibachi

* Sushi

Playlist

"Two Tickets to Paradise" by Eddie Money

"Goodbye My Lover" by James Blunt

"You Oughta Know" by Alanis Morrissette (Kevin breaks out this bad boy with Darryl backing him up on keyboard)

Michael: "Uh-oh. Looks like Santa was a little naughty."

Angela: "What is that?"

Michael: "This is Christmas spirit, as in spirits, booze."

Meredith: "We can drink?"

Toby: "We're really not supposed to serve alcohol."

Michael: "Zip it, Toby! Just . . . I mean, it's a party. Come on. If I can't throw a good party for my employees, then I am a terrible boss. Who wants a drink?"

Meredith: "Me. Please."

Michael: "Go, here we go!"

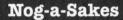

Nog-a-Sakes

Like your friends at Benihana, add a little sake to your holiday get-together.

2 ounces sake
6 ounces eggnog
Nutmeg (optional)

Pour sake and eggnog into a lowball glass over ice. Stir vigorously and sprinkle with nutmeg. Try to remember your date's name—and her face.

Moroccan Christmas

A reminder to remove any trace of a "traditional" Christmas celebration—trees, nativity scenes, mistletoe (you can keep the camels and the North African king), and Santas. This is a Moroccan Christmas.

Phyllis: "This is not your grandmother's Christmas party, unless, of course, she's from Morocco, in which case it's very accurate."

Supplies

* Invitations (required for guests to get in the door)

* Fez hats to distribute

* A sizable number of area rugs and pillows (for seating)

* Genie lamp

* Hookah

* Other forms of entertainment, like belly dancers (note: If one of your colleagues gets too much into the spirit of things, pull the plug on the erotic dance moves)

Menu

* Orange Vodjuiceka (see page 60)

* One-of-Everything (see page 61)

* Phyllis's Hummus and Pita Platter (see page 62)

* Halwa chebakia   * Olives

* Couscous

                    * Kebabs

Playlist

"El-Maddahine (Isawi)" by Chalf Hassan

"Streets of Cairo" (aka "The Snake Charmer Song")

"Deck the Halls" on the sitar

Orange Vodjuiceka

Want to boost that immune system while imbibing a little liquor? It can be done with Michael's Orange Vodjuiceka. It's flavorful, low on carbs, and jam-packed with vitamin C.

Vodka
Orange juice

Pour 2 shots of vodka into a tumbler. Fill to the top of the glass with orange juice and enjoy that flu-fighting cocktail.

Michael: "Jim, Jim . . ."
Jim: "What is it?"
Michael: "That is vodka and I mixed it with orange juice. I call it an orange-vod-juice . . . ka.
Jim: "Wow, that is delicious."
Michael: "Yeah."
Jim: "Can't believe no one's thought of that."
Michael: "I know."
Pam: "You do realize that we can't serve liquor at the party."
Michael: "Yeah, I know. Damn it. Stupid corporate wet blankets. Like booze ever killed anybody."

One-of-Everything

Why settle for just one kind of cocktail when you can have one-of-everything?!

Gin
Scotch
Vermouth
Absinthe
Rum
Triple Sec
Splenda packets

Blend equal parts gin, Scotch, vermouth, absinthe, rum, and triple sec in a shaker. Shake twice. Add two packets of Splenda as a sweet garnish. Call a cab home.

Oscar: "Oh, I haven't bartended in forever. Oh, never considered myself a mixologist. Oh, this is daunting. Um, I'll need a mortar, pestle, muddler . . . does anyone have any chocolate shavings?!"

61

Phyllis's Hummus and Pita Platter

1 cup chickpeas (uncooked, dry)
3 cloves garlic (skins removed and crushed)
⅓ cup tahini
2 tablespoons lemon juice
¾ teaspoon sea salt
1 tablespoon olive oil (or substitute water or more lemon juice)
Pita triangles and crudités (raw cut vegetables), for serving

Optional Additions

¼ teaspoon baking soda (for creamier texture)
1 dash garlic powder
¼ cup fresh herbs (such as cilantro, parsley, or basil)

Place (uncooked) chickpeas in a large pot and cover with 2 inches of water. Bring to a boil over high heat for 1 minute. Cover, remove from heat, and let sit for 1 hour.

Drain and rinse the cooked chickpeas before adding them to a food processor or blender. Blend with garlic, tahini, lemon juice, sea salt, and olive oil. Blend until creamy and smooth, scraping down the sides as needed.

Add any of the optional ingredients, if desired.

Serve with pita and crudités.

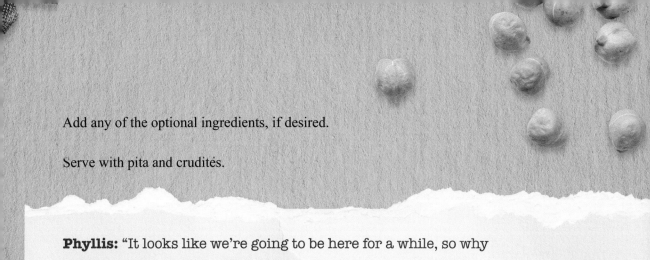

Phyllis: "It looks like we're going to be here for a while, so why don't you make a little plate of hummus for everyone? Little triangles of pita, toasted on both sides, fanned so you can easily grab them."
Angela: "I don't . . ."
Phyllis: "And napkins—fanned."

Classy Christmas

If your coworkers are feeling classy, your boss is a little sassy, and Meredith is acting nasty, have yourself a classy Christmas.

Michael: "Well, this year's gonna be different. We're gonna have fun. It's not gonna be tacky. It's going to be, you know what, the food is going to be austere. It is not going to be tacky deli platter food. It's not gonna have a big, fat, gross Santa Claus. It's gonna be cool, sleek Santa."

Supplies

* Gold, gold, and more gold

* White string lights

Menu

* Wine

* Champagne

* Caviar

* The finest meats and cheeses

* Pam's Box Lasagna (see page 67)

Stanley: "I've been here 18 years and have suffered through some weird thematic Christmases: a Honolulu Christmas, a *Pulp Fiction* Christmas, a Muslim Christmas, Moroccan Christmas, Mo Rocca Christmas . . . I don't want no Kwanzaa wreath, I don't need a dreidel in my face, that's its own thing. And who's that black Santa for? I don't care! I know Santa ain't black! I could care less. I want Christmas! Just give me plain, baby-Jesus-lying-in-a-manger Christmas!"

Playlist

All songs must be performed by a string quartet. If you have budgetary constraints, one member of the quartet will suffice (preferably the bassist).

Holly: "It looks beautiful in here. Super classy. It's like a party for limousine drivers."

STEREO

Pam's Box Lasagna

Pam: "You know, Oscar, every time I make this lasagna people ask me if it's a family recipe, but really, I just get the recipe from the box!"

Take a trip to your local supermarket.

Find the frozen foods aisle.

Scout out a box of premade lasagna and purchase it.

Bake the lasagna at home, transfer it to a nice dish, and pretend you made it from scratch.

Pennsylvania Dutch Christmas

Christmas at Dunder Mifflin is nothing without everyone's favorite assistant (to the) regional manager. Schrutes haven't celebrated birthdays since before the Great Depression, so when it comes to Christmas they go over the top. Here's everything you need to know about hosting your own *das fest*.

Dwight: "No one fears Santa the way they fear Belsnickel."

Jim: "That's my favorite part of Christmas—the authority."

Pam: "And fear."

Supplies

* A personal invitation from Dwight (note: Guests are also expected to follow the Schrute dress code and honor code and pay five Schrute Bucks at the door for entry. Also, no smiling.)

* An authentic suit or whip, canning supplies, and a stick

* A snowball, so you're always prepared for battle

Menu

Playlist

"Various Disgraces" by The Blam

"Wild Side" by Mötley Crüe

"Greensleeves"

"The Longest Time" by "William Joel"

"River Runs Red" by Life of Agony

"Boulevard of Broken Dreams" by Green Day (if you're like Dwight and Andy, then you end the night on a high note, singing about loneliness and destroyed dreams)

Dwight's Special Christmas Goose

Pam: "Merry Christ—NO! Why . . . why did you bring that here?"

Dwight: "Don't worry, she's dead. Oh, wait—he's dead."

Pam: "Dwight, what uh . . ."

Dwight: "I accidentally ran over it. It's a Christmas miracle!"

Pam: "Well, get it out of here."

Dwight: "Relax, okay. And because this is Christmas, I am going to roast this goose and prepare it with a wild rice dressing. Do we have any cayenne pepper in the kitchen?"

4 cups cooked wild rice

⅔ cup chopped hazelnuts

2 Granny Smith apples (peeled, cored, and chopped)

½ cup chopped onion

2 teaspoons ground savory

3 tablespoons chopped fresh parsley

Salt and freshly ground pepper, to taste

12-pound goose

4 cups of water

1 ½ tablespoons all-purpose flour

Mix the cooked rice, nuts, apples, onions, and herbs to create a stuffing. Season to taste with salt and pepper. Preheat the oven to 325°F.

Remove the neck, heart, and gizzard from the goose. Wash the bird inside and out, and pat dry. Fill the cavity of the goose with the stuffing, skewer it closed, and lace butcher's twine around the skewers. Make sure the bird's legs and wings are firmly pressed against the sides to keep the goose from roasting unevenly.

Place the bird breast-side down in the oven and roast for 1 ½ hours. Draw off the fat as it accumulates. Turn it over and roast another 1 ½ hours. When the chicken is done and a meat thermometer reads 165°F, the juices should run clear when the bird is pricked where the thigh attaches to the body. Remove the strings and skewers before carving.

While the goose is roasting, place the neck, heart, and gizzard in a saucepan with the water. Let them simmer gently, partially covered, for several hours, until the liquid is reduced to slightly less than 2 cups. Season the broth to taste with salt.

Pour off all but 1 tablespoon of the fat from the roasting pan. Sprinkle a little flour over the bottom, 1 to 2 tablespoons, depending on how thick you like your gravy. Stir for 2 minutes over low heat, scraping up all the browned bits.

Add the reserved goose broth to the pan and whisk until smooth. Taste and season with salt and pepper.

Dwight: "He was already dead. And we Schrutes use every part of the goose. The meat has a delicious, smoky, rich flavor. Plus, you can use the molten goose grease and save it in the refrigerator, thus saving you a trip to the store for a can of expensive goose grease."

Dwight: "What about an authentic Pennsylvania Dutch Christmas? Drink some Glühwein, enjoy some Hasenpfeffer. Enjoy Christmas with St. Nicholas's rural German companion, Belsnickel."

Glühwein

Glühwein, also known as mulled wine, is a traditional seasonal drink that can be traced all the way back to the 13th century. You might recognize the libation from the likes of Charles Dickens or Christmas markets across the globe.

Meredith: "Ugh. What is this stuff—lava?"
Dwight: "That is Glühwein, otherwise known as glow-wine, also used to sterilize medical instruments. And—interesting factoid—this is the very spoon that guided my soft skull through the birth canal when I was born. Enjoy."

¾ cup water
¾ cup sugar
1 cinnamon stick
1 orange
10 whole cloves
1 bottle red wine

In a saucepan (or a slow cooker), combine the water, sugar, and cinnamon stick over medium heat. Bring to a boil, then turn down the heat and let it simmer.

Cut the orange in half, then squeeze the juice into the pan or the slow cooker. Push the cloves into the outside of the orange peel and place the orange halves in the simmering water mixture. Simmer for 30 minutes, until syrupy.

Add the bottle of red wine and heat until it steams. Remove the orange halves with the embedded cloves. Serve in mugs (cold glasses might break).

Schrute's Apple Strudel

Strudel comes from the German word for "whirlpool" or "eddy" and is a layered pastry with a sweet filling, traditionally apples. Apples vary from firm to semi-firm once baked, with popular varieties including Granny Smith (for a tart strudel) and Golden Delicious (for a sweet strudel).

1 large egg
6 tablespoons sugar, divided
2 teaspoons ground cinnamon, divided
2 ½ cups chopped or sliced apples
Flour, for flouring the work surface
1 sheet frozen puff pastry dough (thawed)

Preheat the oven to 375°F. Beat the egg and 1 tablespoon of water in a small bowl with a fork and set aside.

Mix 3 tablespoons of sugar and 1 teaspoon of cinnamon in a medium bowl. Slowly add the apples and stir to coat.

Sprinkle flour on your work surface and unfold the pastry sheet. Roll the pastry sheet into a 16 x 12-inch rectangle. With the shorter side facing you, spoon the apple mixture onto the bottom half of the pastry sheet. Leave 1 inch around the edge free of filling so you can pinch and seal the strudel later. Roll up like a jelly roll.

With seam-side down, place the rolled dough on a baking sheet. Tuck both ends under to seal. Brush the pastry with the egg mixture and cut several 2- to 3-inch slits in the top of the pastry.

Toss the remaining 1 teaspoon of cinnamon and 3 tablespoons of sugar together in a small bowl and sprinkle over the dough. Bake for 35 minutes or until the pastry is golden brown. Let the pastry cool for 20 minutes, then slice and serve.

DWIGHT SCHRUTE

DETERMINED
WORKER
INTENSE
GOOD WORKER
HARD WORKER
TERRIFIC

Hasenpfeffer

Translated literally as "hare pepper," this dish is sort of like a German ragout and is made with small bits of hare (yes, your small hippity, hoppity friends), cabbage, and potatoes, and stewed for hours. The Schrute family often adds boiled beets to this traditional dish, if their harvest has been plentiful. The Schrutes are well-respected for their roadside beet stands, so adding their award-winning root vegetables to this dish is a real delight.

Hog Maw

In true Pennsylvania Dutch tradition, the Schrutes also serve Hog Maw. The dish, known to few outside of Pennsylvania Dutch country, uses an unconventional part of the pig—its stomach. Stuffed inside of the stomach is a mixture of potatoes, sausage, cabbage, and seasonings.

Kevin: "I love this hog mama."

Phyllis: "Dwight said it's Hog maw."

Kevin: "What is maw?!"

More Schrute Family Christmas Traditions

The Pig Rib

Although this isn't an actual German tradition, it is a tried-and-true Schrute tradition. Once the hog maw has been prepared and devoured by the Schrutes, they use the remains to play a little game. Similar to the traditional "wish bone" game many Americans practice during Thanksgiving, the Schrutes break the ceremonial pig rib. Whoever gets the larger half will have a plentiful harvest in the new year. Dwight's brother Jeb has a solid track record of winning each year. When he plays during the office party, Dwight once again loses, this time to his frenemy Jim.

The Candy Cane, aka Shepherd's Crook

Legend has it that the first candy cane was created around 1670 when a choirmaster in Germany bent sugar-sticks into canes and handed them out to children during the Christmas mass. It wasn't until decades later that the red stripe and peppermint flavoring were added. As time went by, the symbolism and detail grew. Today, many believe the red stripes represent the blood of Christ, while the white space represents his purity. Others believe the *J* shape is an homage to Jesus's name. The only thing we know for sure is that they do not or should not taste like sheep feces.

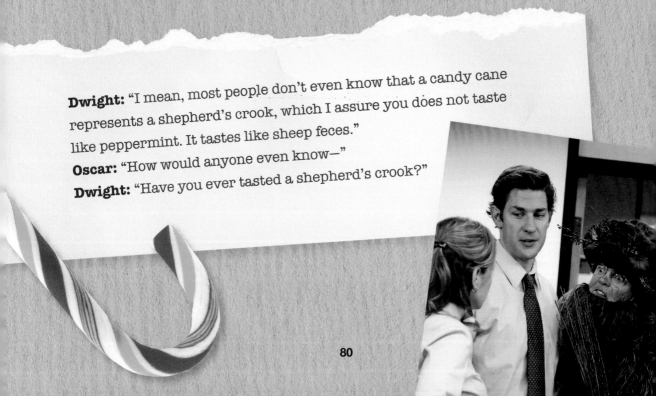

Dwight: "I mean, most people don't even know that a candy cane represents a shepherd's crook, which I assure you does not taste like peppermint. It tastes like sheep feces."

Oscar: "How would anyone even know—"

Dwight: "Have you ever tasted a shepherd's crook?"

Belsnickel

Oscar: "Belsnickel is a crotchety, fur-clad gift giver, related to other companions of St. Nicholas in the folklore of southwestern Germany."

The Schrute version of St. Nick, Belsnickel has been part of the Schrute family Christmas for centuries. Growing up, Dwight's grandfather would play the character, and Dwight has worked to perfect the part ever since. He invested in an authentic suit and whip, and learned enough conversational German to keep the character going for at least an evening.

Each year, Belsnickel visits the boys and girls of Germany (or, in Dwight's case, Dutch country, Pennsylvania) to determine if they've been impish or admirable. Everyone holds out a wooden bowl and waits patiently as Belsnickel determines their fate. If they've been really good, he'll likely gift them fruits and nuts. Other common offerings include canning supplies, a mouse trap, or a stick. If he's deemed them impish, they get a smack from his whip or bristles. Ouch!

Dwight: "Ooh, Belsnickel has traveled from distant lands to discover how all the boys and the girls have been behaving this last year. Whoo hoo HOO hoo hoo! [Runs over to Stanley and points at his stomach with a stick] Ohh . . . too much strudel."

Jim: "So he's kind of like Santa, except dirty and worse."

HOW TO TRIM THE OFFICE TREE

Pam: "Hey, uh, any volunteers to come with me to go buy a Christmas tree?"

Kevin: "I would, but I don't want to get dirty. There might be girls at the party."

* Go big or go home. If the tree is too big, you can cut the top off to form a mini tree that you can then sell to a charity. That's what Christmas is all about.

* Hang pine-scented car air fresheners throughout its branches to give it that freshly cut from the forest smell (even if it's made of plastic).

* Get the whole group involved and plan a tree-trimming afternoon, complete with milk and cookies.

* Have everyone bring in an ornament of their own to personalize the pine tree.

* Host an unveiling ceremony, Rockefeller Center–style.

GIFT GIVING AND HOLIDAY HIGH JINKS

'Tis the season to be pranking! Take a look back at Pam, Jim, and Dwight's best Christmas pranks and get a few ideas of your own. It's not a Dunder Mifflin office party without presents and games—learn how to impress your Christmas crush and what gifts are best avoided.

Michael: "Christmas is awesome. First of all, you get to spend time with the people you love. Secondly, you can get drunk and no one can say anything. Third, you give presents. What's better than giving presents? And fourth, getting presents. So, four things."

DUNDER MIFFLIN GIFT-GIVING WINS AND FAILS

WIN

Over the course of several weeks, Michael gives Dwight pieces of a set that Dwight initially thinks is a gun, but eventually he's able to build the pieces into a nutcracker.

Dwight: "Oh, man! I can use this for so many nuts! Macadamias, Brazil nuts, pecans, almonds. Clams, snails . . ."

WIN

Angela is thrilled with the jazz babies poster that Toby gets for her, and is furious on a future episode when Oscar says the poster is creepy, in bad taste, kitsch, soul-destroying, and more offensive than hardcore porno.

Toby: "I got Angela. She is into these posters of babies dressed as adults. I got her one of those. I felt kind of weird buying that."

WIN

Jim gives Kelly a Robert Pattinson *Twilight* poster, which she loves.

WIN

Kevin draws his own name in Secret Santa and treats himself to a footbath, which he's thrilled with.

Kevin: "I got myself for Secret Santa. I was supposed to tell somebody, but I didn't."

WIN

Kevin gives Oscar UGGS.

Kevin: "For your feet!"

WIN

Phyllis gives Ryan a hand-knitted iPad cover inscribed with his zodiac sign and symbol—Pisces and a fish.

Ryan: "It's amazing. It's so great. Thank you."

WIN

Kelly and Ryan give a pregnant Angela a T-shirt that says, ASK THEN TOUCH.

WIN

Jada gives Michael a vending machine pie.

Darryl: "Hey, Mike."

Michael: "Hey."

Darryl: "We wanted to give you something."

Michael: "Oh."

Jada: "Merry Christmas."

Michael: "Thank you. A Hostess apple pie! This is my favorite breakfast. How did you know that? Thank you very much."

WIN

Jim buys Pam a teapot (so she can make tea at her desk) and fills it with funny items, all meant to remind Pam of their favorite inside jokes. Jim also includes a card, explaining his feelings for her—which he later takes out before she can read it.

WIN

Pam decides to DIY her gift for Jim. She writes and illustrates a comic book based on mild-mannered salesman Jimmy Halpert, who's bitten by a radioactive bear while riding his bike through the forest and becomes Bear Man.

WIN

Pam puts together a hilarious gift for Jim—the ultimate prank on Dwight that she's been working on for months. By sending him fake letters from the CIA, Pam has convinced Dwight that he's been recruited for a secret mission. Jim's gift? To choose his mission.

FAIL

Thrilled to receive his crush, Erin, in the office Secret Santa drawing, Andy decides to go all out and gift her with the 12 Days of Christmas. Unfortunately, Andy learns the hard way that his gift has not been well received.

Erin: "Hello. Sorry, guys. I'm not sure I've earned the right to make announcements yet. But whoever is giving me the "12 Days of Christmas" as my Secret Santa? Please stop. I can't take it anymore. My cat killed a turtledove; the French hens have started pulling out my hair to make a nest. Please. Stop."

$400.00

FAIL

Michael gives Ryan an iPod, which infuriates everyone since they were supposed to keep their spending limit to $20.

Ryan: "Whoa, a video iPod.

Michael: "Whoa. Wow. Jeez. Somebody really got carried away with the spirit of Christmas. That was me. I got a little carried away."

Ryan: "Wasn't there a $20 limit on the gift? This is $400."

Michael: "You don't know that."

Ryan: "Yeah, you left the price tag on."

Michael: "I did?"

FAIL

Creed gives Jim a flannel shirt because he forgot about the gift exchange.

Jim: "He obviously forgot to get me something, and then he went in his closet and dug out this little number and then threw it in a bag."

Creed: "Yep. That's exactly what happened."

FAIL

Oscar gives Creed a keychain.

Oscar: "I got Creed. And, to tell you the truth, I don't know anything about Creed. I know his name's Creed. I know he works right over there. I think he's Irish and I . . . I got him this shamrock keychain."

FAIL

Phyllis gives Michael a handmade oven mitt, leaving him furious.

Michael: "So, Phyllis is basically saying, 'Hey Michael, I know you did a lot to help the office this year but I only care about you a homemade oven mitt's worth.' I gave Ryan an iPod."

FAIL

Dwight gives Michael paintball lessons, which had been intended for Phyllis.

Michael: "Who wants to take paintball lessons? How is that better than an iPod?"

Dwight: "I never said it was better than an iPod."

FAIL

Angela gives Creed deodorant.

96

DUNDER MIFFLIN'S HOLIDAY HIGH JINKS

The Gift-Wrapped Desk

When Dwight arrives at work to find his desk and chair gift-wrapped, he's amused by the thought of how long it must have taken poor, pathetic Jim to get all the wrapping paper on just right. He's feeling rather smug until he sits down in his chair and falls, only to realize that everything has been replaced by cardboard covered in paper.

To recreate this prank, you will need a lot of cardboard and many rolls of festive wrapping paper. Be sure to get the right measurements for your coworker's desk and chair so that it appears they're only gift-wrapped. Then get yourself some recycled cardboard, a ruler, pencil, and glue to create your templates and glue everything together. Don't forget to cover every inch of the cubicle with paper, including notebooks, loose change, and pens.

The Snowball Fight

Jim: "Hey, it's snowing."

Dwight: "Oh my God, it's the first snowfall of Christmas. Is that just so magical for you, little girl? Can you not wait to have a hot chocolate and cuddle up with Papa and tell him about all your Christmas dreams? It's not even a real snow, it's a dusting. Pitiful."

In the midst of Dunder Mifflin's classy Christmas party, Dwight challenges Jim to a snowball war after Jim pegs him in the face with one in the office. What follows is a total bombardment by Dwight, hitting Jim with snowballs throughout the day. As Jim and Pam leave the office at the end of the day, they're met with dozens of eerie snowmen standing in the parking lot, which Jim begins to smash hysterically, thinking Dwight is hiding in one.

To recreate this prank, stockpile a bunch of snowballs in a cooler and be ready to peg your unsuspecting coworker throughout the day—in a meeting, on their bathroom break, when they're on an important call with a client. Finally, recruit other coworkers to help you make a bunch of snowmen in the parking lot, the eerier the better.

The CIA Assignment

As a Christmas gift for Jim, Pam has led Dwight to believe for months that he's being recruited by the CIA.

To recreate this prank, make an official-looking template marked "classified" and pick a coworker to be your target. On week one, use the template to write up a story that your coworker is being recruited for a top-secret mission and must perform a new task every week to be considered for the job. Once a week, write up a different task for your coworker to perform. Tasks might include moving a coworker's desk and chair into the bathroom or putting another coworker's stapler in Jell-O. For the last week, write to your coworker one last time telling them that another person has been chosen for the job, but they came really close.

LASSIFIED

The Prank War

Jim: "So Dwight did take the bait. He used my credit card numbers to send a $200 bouquet of flowers to my wife . . . from me."

After Dwight and Jim's new desk mate, Cathy, grows tired of their antics, Andy tells them they need to call a halt to their pranks or risk losing their Christmas bonuses.

To recreate this prank, you'll want to pretend that one of your coworkers has it out for you by pulling a series of pranks on yourself, such as: Put a porcupine in your desk drawer, so that when you open it you'll prick your hand and can blame your coworker; deface a photo of your child or loved one and blame it on your coworker; spray-paint your own car with [YOUR NAME] SUCKS and blame it on your coworker.

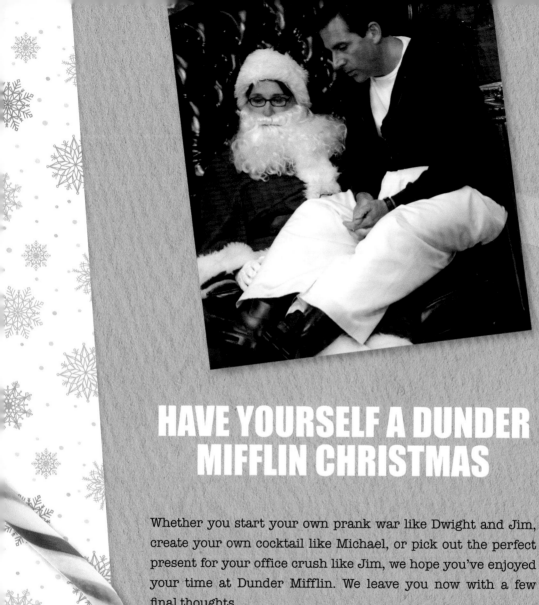

HAVE YOURSELF A DUNDER MIFFLIN CHRISTMAS

Whether you start your own prank war like Dwight and Jim, create your own cocktail like Michael, or pick out the perfect present for your office crush like Jim, we hope you've enjoyed your time at Dunder Mifflin. We leave you now with a few final thoughts.

25 DAYS OF DUNDER MIFFLIN CHRISTMAS

Now that you've relived all the amazing memories (and painful moments) from all seven Christmas episodes, it's time to plan your own calendar of activities to celebrate the 25 Days of Christmas *The Office* way. We encourage you to create your own list and include your officemates in on the fun. To help you get started, we suggest organizing a Yankee Swap/Nasty Christmas/White Elephant or Secret Santa; have a good old-fashioned snowball fight or build a snowman (a friendly one, not one of Dwight's nightmare-inducing creations), book a getaway for the upcoming year (Sandals, anyone?), throw your own annual office Christmas bash, treat yourself (to a footbath, to a cookie, to whatever you want), and finally, spend time with the ones you love—or love to hate.

A MERRY DUNDER MIFFLIN CHRISTMAS

We hope you've enjoyed reliving some of your favorite Christmas episodes from *The Office* and that we've inspired you to start a new holiday tradition, whether that's throwing an epic office party, performing a Christmas karaoke duet, or dressing up as Jesus, Santa, or Belsnickel. And remember, no matter how much you may want to, you can't actually cancel Christmas, and presents will always be the best way to show someone you care. For now, we wish a very merry Dunder Mifflin Christmas to all, and to all a good night!